MAD MARY

WORKBOOK

LIZ CURTIS HIGGS

WATERBROOK
PRESS

MAD MARY WORKBOOK
PUBLISHED BY WATERBROOK PRESS
2375 Telstar Drive, Suite 160
Colorado Springs, Colorado 80920
A division of Random House, Inc.

ISBN 1-57856-632-0

Printed in the United States of America
2002—First Edition

10 9 8 7 6 5 4 3 2 1

CONTENTS

MAD ABOUT MARY MAGDALENE

Welcome, my sister, to a decidedly different way of studying Scripture! You're about to meet *two* Mary Magdalenes: first, a contemporary, fictional one from modern Chicago; then a historical, biblical one from ancient Magdala. Both Marys have much to teach us about what it means to be transformed when Christ appears at the threshold of a woman's heart.

Of all the women whose lives I studied for *Bad Girls of the Bible* and *Really Bad Girls of the Bible,* Mary Magdalene was the one who most captured my imagination. What a woman! My hope is that you, too, will be inspired by Mary M.'s story through the pages of *Mad Mary* and that this companion workbook will enhance your learning, growing experience.

Maybe you plan to read and study *Mad Mary* with some friends from church or work—terrific! For the next six weeks or so, consider me an "invisible" member of your group, speaking to you through these workbook pages, encouraging you to glean all you can from this incredible woman's journey of faith.

My recommendation? Read all the way through the first half of *Mad Mary*— the modern Mary Margaret Delaney's story—before you open the workbook. Fiction allows us to climb inside a character's heart, seeing the world through her eyes and sharing her every emotion, so that her discoveries become our own and the lessons she learns speak to our lives as well.

Then it's time to move from "The Story" to "The Study," which explores, verse by verse, the real Mary Magdalene's life as recorded in the Bible. The questions at the end of each chapter of the *Mad Mary* study section are included (and expanded) in this workbook, with plenty of room for writing down your answers and observations. You'll find it easiest to read the whole chapter first, then go back and answer the corresponding workbook questions.

In fact, why not keep things simple and answer one or two questions per day, one chapter per week? That way you'll be all set for your weekly gathering without a lot of last-minute scribbling. (Been there, babe!) If you're studying *Mad Mary* on your own, following this plan will prepare you to move on to the next chapter, knowing you've truly learned something about yourself and about this unique woman in Jesus' life.

Now, suppose we get started. In addition to this companion workbook, you'll need: (1) your own copy of the book *Mad Mary*, (2) your favorite Bible (any translation is fine—I used the *New International Version*), and (3) your favorite pen. I'd urge you to let go of any concerns about finding that one "correct" answer to the questions that follow, and instead approach things with an open heart and a teachable spirit, making growth in Christ your primary goal.

As you read and study, may you be transformed into a woman as bold as Mary Magdalene, who declared without apology, "I have seen the Lord!"

"Wow...Liz did it again. The Holy Spirit has done a great work in the lives of the women in my class through *Mad Mary*. Feelings and emotions are running high each week of our study and transformation has taken place. Mary Magdalene is my favorite woman in the Bible!"

Lois from California

ONE

HER INFINITE VARIETY

Her Legend

Mary of Magdala is legendary, all right…ooh, baby, the stories we've heard! But *why* is she so famous and *what* can we learn from her? That's what this chapter is all about. We'll check out the myth-conceptions that have swirled around Mary Magdalene for the last two thousand years and discover how those rumors got started. But since it's the biblical Mary M. who matters most, that's where we'll begin.

1a. When Mary Magdalene is introduced in Luke 8, she's listed among those who were followers of Jesus. Some of them—like the Twelve—were called to follow him while others followed by their own choice. Read **Matthew 4:18-22** and **Matthew 9:9.** What were these five men doing when they were called by Jesus?

b. How did the men respond to his invitation?

c. You'll find yet another invitation offered in **John 1:43.** As with the other five men, did Philip seek out Jesus…or did Jesus go looking for Philip?

d. When you first considered following Christ and his teachings, were you actively seeking him…or did you sense that he'd been seeking you? What prompts you to believe that?

e. Jot down what the following verses reveal to you about *seeking:*

Luke 19:10

Acts 17:26-27

Hebrews 11:6

f. Though we have no record of Mary Magdalene's seeking out Jesus or being called to follow him, she clearly chose to do so. Read **Luke 8:1-3.** List all those who are mentioned as followers.

g. Would Jesus' relationships with both groups—the twelve male disciples and Jesus' many female followers—be of equal value and importance to him, do you suppose? Why do you think he included both men and women in his ministry?

h. How might **Acts 5:14** and **1 Corinthians 12:4-6** help answer that question?

Mary Magdalene is neither the first nor the last woman in history to suffer from a bad—but false—reputation.

Liz Curtis Higgs in *Mad Mary*, page 151

2a. Before you read *Mad Mary,* how would you have described Mary Magdalene?

b. Where did those ideas and images come from?

c. One of the women whose story has become entangled with Mary M.'s appears in **Luke 7:36-50.** Skim through those verses, then note in what ways her story matches the popular—though not biblical—image of Mary Magdalene.

d. Some people have assumed the story found in **John 8:1-11** refers to Mary M. Again, what aspects of this nameless woman's story do you think have been falsely attributed to Mary Magdalene?

e. The fact that the gospel writers referred to Mary *by name* tells us that Mary of Magdala was a significant figure among Christ's followers. Read **Luke 8:1-3** again. What facts *do* we know, absolutely, about Mary Magdalene from these verses?

f. Why is it important to have an honest understanding of Mary Magdalene...or for that matter, any biblical character?

g. How does our view of the unique people found in Scripture reflect...

how we see ourselves?

how we see others?

how we see the Christ?

h. Just as Mary M. has been misunderstood over the centuries, so do we some-times misjudge or mistreat our own brothers and sisters in Christ. How do the following verses guide us in our attitude toward others?

Galatians 6:10

Titus 3:1-2

1 John 4:21

Mary Magdalene deserves an honest bio. And we deserve a gutsy role model.

Liz Curtis Higgs in *Mad Mary,* page 145

3a. How is Hollywood responsible, in part, for keeping Mary Magdalene's Bad Girl myth alive? To what end?

b. Have you seen any of the movies mentioned in *Mad Mary* on pages 146-147 or others that included Mary Magdalene? If so, what do you remember about her role?

c. What other media influences come to mind concerning Mary's history—artwork, television programs, books? In what ways did they refute or reinforce her Bad Girl image?

d. What should be the Christian's response to the media's mishandling of biblical stories? Do we raise the roof, refuse to support their advertisers, or hope they just go away?

e. Summarize the following verses, which describe what our conduct should be in such situations.

2 Corinthians 4:1-2

2 Timothy 2:15

1 Peter 2:12

f. The next time you observe popular culture and scriptural truth colliding, would you be willing to e-mail the television station, write the newspaper editor, call the radio talk show? If so, what would you say? What are some practical, redemptive ways to respond?

It wasn't only the Twelve who kept Jesus company. Some *women* followed him too.   Liz Curtis Higgs in *Mad Mary,* page 141

4a. In the book of Proverbs you'll find many references to Bad Girls…specifically, prostitutes and adulteresses. Read **Proverbs 6:25-26; 7:10-12; 7:25-27;** and **23:26-28** for apt descriptions of wanton women who entrap willing victims. Though *men* are the ones who fall for their cunning ways, we generally speak of "fallen women" and not "fallen men." Why is that, do you suppose? How might that explain why people have been so quick to paint Mary Magdalene as a scarlet woman?

 b. Does society seem to expect more of women, morally and spiritually? What evidence do you find to support your answer?

 c. If you see a similar double standard among Christians—an assumption that women should be more righteous or holy than men—is that expectation biblical? Why or why not?

d. Although there do seem to be more stories in the New Testament about Bad Girls who were pardoned by Jesus than there are about Bad Boys who sought his forgiveness, you'll find a prime example of such a fella in **Luke 19:1-10.** What makes Zacchaeus a sinner, and how does Jesus demonstrate grace to him?

e. In particular, **Luke 19:10** is a powerful reminder of why Jesus came. Write it out here, first in his words, then in your own words as this verse applies to your own life.

f. What does **Romans 3:9-11** assure us is true about men and women, Jews and Gentiles... in fact, about *all* people?

g. **Romans 3:23** is a sobering reminder. What does that verse mean to you personally?

It's not by accident that Mary Magdalene is mentioned before the others.

Liz Curtis Higgs in *Mad Mary,* page 142

5a. Not only do we need a new view of Mary M.'s reputation, we also need to take a second look at her birth certificate. What age do *you* think Mary Magdalene was when she joined Jesus' ministry team? What makes you say that?

b. On pages 148-149 you'll find four reasons why I'm convinced Mary Magdalene was older than her Hollywood image. Which one of those reasons rings most true to you, and why?

c. How might it change your perception of her—and identification with her—if she was indeed middle-aged or older?

d. Honesty check: Do you ever find yourself in some way judging, belittling, ignoring, or distancing yourself from those who are significantly older than you? Describe your thoughts and feelings.

e. Read **Leviticus 19:32** and **Proverbs 16:31.** According to Scripture, what should our attitude be toward those around us who are "well seasoned"?

f. Based on **Job 12:12,** how might an older woman have served as an ideal support person for Jesus' ministry?

g. Does it matter what age Mary Magdalene was? Why or why not?

One source of the confusion is simply this: too many Marys.

Liz Curtis Higgs in *Mad Mary,* page 142

6a. Magdala was a town known for immorality. How might that have impacted Mary M.'s reputation in the first century?

b. Jesus' hometown didn't earn him any respect either. Read **John 1:45-46.** Despite Jesus' impressive list of credentials, what is Nathanael's assumption about people from Nazareth?

c. How might Jesus' statement in **Mark 6:4** apply to Mary Magdalene as well?

d. Below you'll find a list of modern cities. Next to each one, jot down a word or two that describes how you might expect the people who live there to behave. Go with the first thing that pops into your mind, even if it's a stereotype.

Las Vegas

Tokyo

Dallas

London

San Francisco

Paris

Detroit

Rome

e. Any negatives appear on your list? If so, what do you think has influenced your opinion?

f. What do the following verses teach us about those negative judgments?

Matthew 7:1-2

Romans 14:10

g. How might such global misconceptions affect our willingness to evangelize, fellowship with, or serve others?

h. Read **Acts 10:34-35.** What are some practical steps we can take to overcome our geographical prejudices both at home and abroad?

Are *you* willing to see her as she was—a woman possessed by Satan, then repossessed by Christ?   Liz Curtis Higgs in *Mad Mary*, page 147

7a. Satan loves nothing more than tearing down God's people. We learn in **1 Peter 5:8** that we are to be on the alert for his schemes. If indeed the Adversary *is* to blame for our myth-understandings about Mary Magdalene, what might he be trying to accomplish?

b. Yet another honesty check: Are you disappointed (even a little) that Mary M. wasn't *that kind* of Bad Girl? Why or why not?

c. Has blurring the truth about Mary's life hurt Christian women specifically? If so, how?

d. How does **Romans 16:17-18** address that question?

e. How could revealing the truth about Mary Magdalene bring about something good for God's kingdom?

f. If you're ready to wipe the slate clean and meet the real Mary Magdalene, what do you hope to learn about this ancient, biblical sister?

What *is* the world coming to? It's coming to *grace*.

Liz Curtis Higgs in *Mad Mary*, page 141

8a. Turn to chapters 1 and 2 in the "Story" section of *Mad Mary*. Do you remember how you felt toward Mary Delaney when you *first* read the opening pages? Jot down what you recall of your *initial* reaction to her, scene by scene.

SCENE   YOUR FIRST IMPRESSION
                                                 OF MARY DELANEY

Jake meets her on the street *(page 1)*

Mary walks through her house *(page 10)*

Mary visits the graveyard *(page 15)*

Jake finds her at Lincoln Park *(page 25)*

Jake comes to take her home *(page 37)*

b. Assuming you've already read Mary Delaney's story all the way through, how have your feelings changed about her as you look back over these early scenes...and why?

c. What does Pastor Jake Stauros *do* and *say* in these first two chapters that reflects his Christlike nature?

d. On page 16 we're briefly introduced to Charles Farris. Who might Charles represent from biblical times? (Hint: On the church roster, his name is listed as "Farris, C."…!) Read **Matthew 9:11-12; 23:13.** How do those words of Jesus apply to this story and to Charles Farris in particular?

e. What has Mary Delaney's story taught you about our very human tendency to discount people who are "different" or to believe the worst about them?

f. In what ways does this modern retelling of Mary's story help you understand the historical Mary Magdalene's life before Jesus delivered her from those seven demons?

Two

Moonstruck Madness

Her Demons

T rue confession: During the research phase of *Mad Mary,* I toyed with skipping all this nasty demon business. After all, Mary Magdalene is set free from them by the time we meet her. Why not ignore these bad boys and move on? The answer is twofold: (1) Mary is the only demoniac in the New Testament who is named and whose demons are numbered. That's significant, babe. And (2) her hellish past makes her heavenly future all the more glorious. Fear not, then. Her seven demons will soon be history.

1a. Read **Luke 8:2** and **Mark 16:9.** Were you aware, before beginning this study, that Mary of Magdala was demon possessed until she met Jesus? And what does that phrase "demon possessed" mean to you?

b. Do you think it's possible for Mary M. to have been possessed without somehow inviting those demons in? Why or why not?

c. Check out the last paragraph on page 157 of *Mad Mary*. What evidence do I offer that suggests possessed people were not responsible for their demonic state?

d. List several truths that the following verses teach you about Jesus' ability to deliver people from spiritual bondage.

Mark 1:27

Luke 6:17-19

1 John 3:8

e. Read **Luke 11:24-26.** Once Jesus cast out the demons, what did he caution his followers against?

f. Then what *should* believers be filled with? The following verses point us in the right direction.

Romans 15:13

Ephesians 5:18

g. Why do you think the details of Jesus' casting out Mary Magdalene's seven demons were not included in any of the four gospels?

h. Does the fact that her deliverance is not described in Scripture make you doubt the reality of it? Why or why not?

When we invite Christ into our hearts, his dwelling place, *he will not share his lodging with demons.*   Liz Curtis Higgs in *Mad Mary*, page 159

2a. Do you believe in literal demons? On what do you base your conclusion?

b. How do the following verses help answer that question for you?

Matthew 8:31-32

Matthew 12:28

Mark 9:25

c. We're taught in **1 John 4:1-6** to "test the spirits." According to those verses, how can we tell the difference between godly spirits and evil ones?

d. For those who know Christ as Savior, how do the following verses assure us we are truly safe—internally and eternally—from evil spirits?

John 10:27-29

1 John 5:18-20

e. Read the section called "The Girl Can't Help It..." on pages 158-159 of *Mad Mary.* Have you ever blamed the Adversary for your sin habits? Are there besetting sins in your life you need to confess? Don't be afraid, beloved. Just write them down.

f. Now the good news: What hope does **1 John 4:9-10** offer sinners like us?

g. According to **Romans 8:35-37,** from what will we *never* be separated?

h. Read **Romans 8:38-39** aloud. Has any stone been left unturned—"death nor life," "height nor depth"—any possibility not been covered?

i. Is *feeling* separated from God the same as *being* separated from him? Why or why not?

j. When we feel distant from the Lord, where can we turn for help and assurance? What does **Hebrews 10:22-23** encourage us to do?

k. Read **Ephesians 2:13.** What makes closeness to God possible?

Two thousand years ago Mary Magdalene wasn't a Bad Girl...she was a Mad Girl.   Liz Curtis Higgs in *Mad Mary,* page 155

3a. Read **Mark 5:2-5** and the parallel passage in **Luke 8:27.** It's difficult to imagine the demoniac as naked and shrieking and abusing himself in the desert...and to think of Mary Magdalene perhaps doing the very same things. Although mental illness and demon possession are by no means the same, they *looked* the same to people in the first century. How do we handle such behaviors in our own century?

b. On pages 161-162 of *Mad Mary,* I described my own encounter with an apparent "Mad Mary." Have you had a comparable experience? If so, what thoughts and feelings confronted you at the time?

c. Are mentally ill people somehow to blame for their illness? Why or why not?

d. How might you comfort their family members? What help might **2 Corinthians 1:3-4** be to you—and to them—in such a situation?

e. Are you confident that Christ offers hope for *all* who are hurting? What makes you say that? And what is that hope?

f. What do the following verses teach us about God's awareness of and provision for those who are in some way afflicted?

Psalm 22:24

Psalm 72:12-14

Isaiah 49:13

Welcome to *grace*. It's the last place a demon wants to hang out.

Liz Curtis Higgs in *Mad Mary,* page 159

4a. Read the section called "Deliverance 101" on pages 163-164 of *Mad Mary,* then answer the following questions about Jesus' methods of healing illnesses and delivering demons.

Who came to Jesus?

What time of day did they come?

How did Jesus *heal* the sick?

How did he *deliver* the demon possessed?

b. Read **Matthew 8:16.** What does the statement "he drove out the spirits with a word" tell us about the power of Christ's spoken words?

c. How do the following verses describe "the word" of God?

John 1:1

John 15:3

Colossians 1:25-27

d. Read the deliverance stories in **Mark 9:17-27** and **Luke 4:33-37.** Did the demons have a choice to obey or disobey Jesus? What makes you say that?

e. According to **Ephesians 6:11,** what must we do to keep the Adversary at arm's length?

f. Now read **2 Corinthians 10:4-5.** Where do these verses suggest that the greatest battles occur?

g. Write here a brief prayer—a word or two—you can quickly send heaven-ward when you find yourself under attack from those pernicious spirits.

h. Read **Ephesians 6:12-17.** According to these verses, what do Christians have as a ready defense against the Adversary? How could you *put on* these five forms of spiritual armor and *put to use* your one powerful weapon?

	SPIRITUAL ARMOR	PRACTICAL IDEAS FOR PUTTING IT ON
Verse 14		
Verse 14		
Verse 15		
Verse 16		
Verse 17		

	ONE WEAPON	PRACTICAL IDEAS FOR PUTTING IT TO USE
Verse 17		

i. Again, prayer is a vital part of our defense. What does Jesus ask the Lord to do on our behalf in **Matthew 6:13,** a verse from what is commonly known as the Lord's Prayer?

j. And what encouragement is offered in **2 Thessalonians 3:1-3?**

> His spoken word had the authority, the energy, the ability to change
> everything.   Liz Curtis Higgs in *Mad Mary*, page 168

5a. Using a good dictionary, jot down an official definition for the word
supernatural.

b. Has there been a specific incident in your life, a particular moment, when
you were aware of something happening outside the natural realm? If so,
describe it.

c. Does it comfort you—or frighten you—to think of a spiritual world outside
of our own earthly experience? Why do you say that?

d. Read **Colossians 1:13-17,** which not only affirms that a spiritual realm exists but also that Christ has dominion over it. How do the following verses further assure you that our "invisible God" reigns supreme?

Ephesians 1:18-21

Hebrews 1:3

Jude 24-25

e. Read the words recorded by Paul, spoken to him by Jesus, in **Acts 26:17-18.** Note the order of things in verse 18: First our eyes must be *opened,* then our heads, hearts, and lives must be *turned* in the opposite—and correct—direction. Who or what can open our eyes so that we see not only this physical world but the spiritual realm around us as well? And who or what will turn us in the right direction?

f. How is Mary Magdalene's life an ideal example of *both* those kingdoms—darkness and light—and what did it take for her eyes to be opened and her life to be turned around?

Demons were real, and Jesus had dominion over them.

Liz Curtis Higgs in *Mad Mary,* page 161

6a. Take a brief look at some of the people Jesus delivered and healed during his earthly ministry. Jot down how each of these afflicted men responded—what they did or what they said—when Jesus made them whole.

THEIR RESPONSE

Matthew 9:27-31   The Blind Men

Matthew 9:32-33   The Mute Man

Luke 17:12-14   The Leprous Men

b. As you continue reading **Luke 17:15-19,** you'll discover that, of those ten who were healed of leprosy, only one man returned to offer thanks. What does that suggest to you about this story in particular and human nature in general?

c. Why do you suppose the dozens—even hundreds—of people whom Jesus healed and delivered didn't come forward in his defense during his last days?

d. **Colossians 3:17** bids us to be grateful and give Jesus honor where honor is due, yet so often one answer to prayer simply produces another request. Think of a recent circumstance where God intervened on your behalf. What was your response?

e. What do you need to thank the Lord for right now? Has he delivered you, healed you, forgiven you, cleansed you, blessed you, and/or guided you in some way? Read **Psalm 31:7-8,** then put your gratitude in writing as a note of thanks addressed to Jesus.

> How sweet the sound of his voice must have been to the mad who became suddenly sane at his appearing.   Liz Curtis Higgs in *Mad Mary,* page 175

7a. Read the story of the Gerasene demoniac and his deliverance in **Mark 5:1-20.** You'll notice in verse 18 that the man asked to join Jesus, to no avail. List some reasons why you think Jesus didn't allow the delivered demoniac to climb in his boat and follow him.

b. How do you think the man felt when he was sent back to his family...
disappointed? angry? humbled? grateful? Why do you say that?

c. Yet Jesus permitted Mary and the other women to follow him. Why, do
you suppose?

d. Have you ever questioned why God seemed to have one calling on your life
but another on someone else's? If so, describe your struggle...and what you
learned from it.

e. How would sending the demon-delivered man back to his community...

benefit his family?

bless his community?

serve the kingdom of God?

f. According to the following verses, what clearly makes the difference in our ability to testify to the truth of the gospel?

Matthew 10:18-20

Acts 1:8

1 Thessalonians 1:4-7

No one—and no thing—would ever stake a claim on Mary Magdalene again.

Liz Curtis Higgs in *Mad Mary*, page 176

8a. Read again chapters 3 and 4 in the "Story" part of *Mad Mary* with the following questions in mind. How does the opening epigraph on page 39 about the "power of the visible" parallel the truth found in **Colossians 1:15?**

b. Make a note of the specific ways in which Pastor Jake's "church planting" ministry mirrors that of the Christ whom he serves.

c. What small but significant risks does Jake take on Mary Delaney's behalf… and what motivates Jake to take those risks? In what ways does **Ephesians 5:1-2** explain Jake's method of ministry?

d. Why do you think Mary Delaney rejects his ministry at first? And how do you relate to Mary's resistance—or Jake's persistence—in some personal way?

e. Jake's sermon on pages 52-53 is based on **Luke 13:10-16.** Take a moment to read the Scripture, then read this brief scene again. How does this message speak to you?

f. Write out the old Irish proverb that Mary Delaney recalls, as noted on page 56, then below it write **Acts 3:19.** What significance might these words about "turning" have for you?

THREE

THROUGH THICK AND THIN
Her Dedication

Throughout the earthly ministry of Christ, the one word that rings like the peal of the Liberty Bell itself is *freedom.* He set people free from their pasts, free from their demons, free from their illnesses, free from their sins, and free from the Law so they might embrace the Spirit. Our sister Mary Magdalene understood better than most the blessing—and the cost—of that freedom.

1a. Read once more **Luke 8:1-3.** It seems Mary Magdalene hung out with other demon-delivered and disease-freed women—Joanna and Susanna, to name two. Do you find yourself drawn to those whose backgrounds are similar to yours—whether strait-laced, sin filled, or somewhere in the middle—or do you seek out people with decidedly different backgrounds? Why is that the case, do you think?

b. What are the advantages and disadvantages of surrounding yourself with women who have very different spiritual backgrounds? What does **Romans 14:13** tell us to do?

c. How do the following verses encourage, even challenge you to treat your brothers and sisters in Christ, no matter what their circumstances, past or present?

John 13:34-35

Romans 12:10

Romans 12:16

d. How does God demonstrate his willingness to reach people from all walks of life, as recorded in these passages?

Isaiah 57:15

Luke 15:7

Galatians 3:28

e. How might **Psalm 142:7** parallel Mary M.'s life among the followers of Christ?

f. According to the following verses, how did his followers help one another …and how can we do the same today?

Romans 15:14

Colossians 3:16

g. **Ephesians 4:11-13** describes the distribution of spiritual gifts among believers, including the gift of teaching. Imagine Mary Magdalene as your Bible study leader and the unique background she would bring to her teaching. How can people with checkered pasts have a special teaching ministry today?

h. For those who teach the Bible, what cautions do the following verses offer for handling the inevitable conflicts that drag our attention away from God's truth?

2 Timothy 2:23-26

2 Timothy 4:2-5

James 3:1-2

This wasn't a job or a ministerial appointment for Mary. It was a commitment as binding as marriage, and it cost her everything.

Liz Curtis Higgs in *Mad Mary*, page 181

2a. On page 181 of *Mad Mary* I suggest several possible reasons Mary M. left the life that she had known in Magdala, following her deliverance. Why do *you* think she left Magdala? Was she running away from her past—or toward her future? What makes you say that?

b. What comparisons can you make between Paul's statement in **Philippians 3:13-14** and Mary Magdalene's dedication to the Christ?

c. Sometimes moving forward with Jesus means leaving behind our favorite sins. In **John 8:9-11,** Jesus extends forgiveness to a sinful woman caught in adultery. What does he command her to do? Do you think she obeyed him? Why would you say that?

d. Read **Colossians 3:7-10.** What are you learning to leave behind in your pursuit of Christ?

e. What has been difficult about doing that?

f. What has made it worth the sacrifice?

g. How do the following verses encourage you?

Jeremiah 29:11

Ephesians 3:16-19

h. What have you learned in the process of letting go and pressing on?

The women followed Jesus out of sheer love and gratitude.

Liz Curtis Higgs in *Mad Mary,* page 182

3a. Jesus came to set people free, and that included women. Read the two
parables he shares in **Luke 15:3-10.** What lessons do these two stories teach?
Do they seem to carry equal weight? If not, how do they differ? And if they
are essentially the same, then why two parables instead of just one?

b. Read page 183 in *Mad Mary.* Those restrictions for women in Mary's time and place sound extreme to us two thousand years later. Might any have been valid for that era? And were those reasons spiritual in nature or merely practical…or both?

c. Do you see any social or cultural restrictions for women today (unwritten but understood) like those described in the above passage? If so, name one or two. What reasons are typically given for those limitations?

d. Read **1 Corinthians 11:11-12** and **Ephesians 5:21.** Do you think men in ancient Judea and Galilee responded differently than women did to Christ's equal-opportunity ministry? What makes you say that?

e. In our own day and age, what differences do you see in how men and women respond to the Lord Jesus and his teachings?

f. On page 184 of *Mad Mary*, we read about Jerome and others who vehemently opposed women serving as leaders in the early church. Perhaps you've heard similar statements (minus the anger!) in recent times. How would you respond to them?

If we want all that Jesus has to offer us, we gotta be willing to give him everything first.   Liz Curtis Higgs in *Mad Mary*, page 195

4a. We've met Mary the demon-possessed madwoman, Mary the educated woman of means, and now Mary the woman who gave it all up for God. How do you reconcile such different personas?

b. Name some people you've known who, over the course of time, have lived very different lives. What—or who—changed them, and how did that process take place?

c. How does **2 Corinthians 5:17** help explain drastic identity shifts like these? In what ways does a person become a "new creation"?

d. What reaction have you seen in people as they "meet" Jesus for the first time? How is their perspective different from the perspective of those who have grown up knowing about Jesus?

e. Read **Matthew 18:1-4.** On this occasion, Jesus taught his followers what having a change of heart would require. What do you think the Lord means by asking us to be "childlike"?

f. One of the qualities we cherish in young children is their innocence. How does **Ephesians 4:22-24** teach us that even those of us who've "been there, done that" can be made brand-new?

g. What steps can we take to embrace a new view of ourselves and others who've had a life-changing encounter with Christ?

Unless we compare every teaching to the revealed Word of God, we run the risk of being pulled in the wrong direction.

Liz Curtis Higgs in *Mad Mary,* page 195

5a. Before beginning this study, were you familiar with the Nag Hammadi papyrus books unearthed last century, as described on page 188 of *Mad Mary?* What was your initial reaction to these ancient texts?

b. Do such texts, some of which contradict the biblical canon, challenge or threaten your faith? Why or why not?

c. Should we give genuine ancient texts like these equal weight with Scripture? What prompts you to say that?

d. Read the following verses and note what they tell us about the Word of God.

Psalm 119:89

Isaiah 55:10-11

Hebrews 4:12

e. How would you respond to someone who believes differently than you do on the authority of the Bible? What do the following verses suggest?

2 Timothy 3:16-17

2 Peter 1:20-21

f. Read **1 Peter 1:23-25.** Why is the Word of God so important?

It seems Mary was as willing to go against convention as Jesus was.

Liz Curtis Higgs in *Mad Mary,* page 187

6a. Reread pages 189-191 of *Mad Mary,* finishing at "No further debate needed." Was it ever your understanding that Jesus and Mary were more than friends, that they were attracted to one another or were, in fact, lovers? What might have been the origin of that notion?

b. Since Mary Magdalene was merely human—and *not* divine—might there have been a one-sided attraction on her part, do you think? How might **Ephesians 5:3** answer that question?

c. If you'd not previously heard of such a theory, linking Mary M. and Jesus in an intimate relationship, does the conjecture surprise you? disgust you? intrigue you? In what ways would it undermine your faith—as well as the ministry of Christ—if it *were* true?

d. What does **Hebrews 4:15** tell us about Jesus and fleshly temptations?

e. What assurance do you find in **Hebrews 7:26** and **James 1:13** that Jesus would never have engaged in such a relationship with Mary M.?

f. Read **1 Thessalonians 4:3-7.** How do these verses let us confidently put aside any concerns of this nature?

Mary Magdalene's contribution to Jesus' ministry flat *counted.*

Liz Curtis Higgs in *Mad Mary*, page 182

7a. Mary Magdalene was both a follower and a leader. How is that possible? Aren't these traits opposites?

b. Do you lean toward following or leading—or do you demonstrate both skills, as Mary M. did? Think of an example from your own life when, due to particular circumstances, it would be prudent to be a leader. And then think of one where it would be better to be a follower.

c. As the old nursery rhyme (almost) says, "Everywhere the Lamb went, Mary was sure to go!" What does **John 10:3-5** reveal about our Shepherd and about us, his sheep?

d. Following Christ can and will cost us everything. **Matthew 10:37-39** is a very challenging passage, sis! How do those verses apply to your life right now?

e. Read **John 12:26; Philippians 2:3;** and **James 4:10.** Servanthood and humility are seldom part of our twenty-first-century vocabulary. Why are those qualities essential for those who want to follow Christ?

f. Read **John 6:66** and **Matthew 26:55-56.** Why did Jesus' disciples stop following him? Fear of death? of looking foolish? What possible explanations would you offer?

g. Do any of those reasons you listed above mirror why people turn away from Christ's message today? Underline the ones that are still stumbling blocks for the people you care about.

h. We have no record of Mary Magdalene's doubting or challenging or denying the Christ. If doubt or denial of the truths of Christianity ever invades your own heart, how could Mary M. serve as a role model for you?

i. Write out the words of the apostle Paul in **1 Timothy 1:12.** Mary's life demonstrated the same level of gratitude and commitment. In what ways are you prepared to follow her example?

Women could defend him, support him, follow him...but they could not save him.   Liz Curtis Higgs in *Mad Mary*, page 194

8a. Read again chapters 5 and 6 of *Mad Mary.* What milestones mark Mary's change from a madwoman to a glad woman in the following scenes?

FROM MAD MARY TO GLAD MARY

in Jake's office *(pages 79-80)*

at St. Clement Church *(pages 82-83)*

with the Sisters *(page 85)*

in Luna's old room *(page 91)*

at the estate sale *(page 93)*

at Calvary Fellowship *(page 98)*

b. By the end of chapter 6 (pages 107-108), Glad Mary turns into Sad Mary. When you initially read the story, what did you think might be coming next for Jake...and for Mary?

c. How do any emotions stirred by our modern Mary's story help you relate to ancient Mary Magdalene who also spent a very dark Friday watching her beloved teacher die?

d. What made the disciples feel sad at the Last Supper, according to **Matthew 26:21-22?**

e. Mary Magdalene did not betray her Lord...but I have. Many times, in small but sadly significant ways. By not speaking out, by not taking a stand, by not denouncing sin when I see it. If you, too, have ever betrayed the Lord in some manner, what would you like to say to him now?

Four

PATH OF SORROW

Her Despair

I n the opening paragraphs of chapter 12 in *Mad Mary,* I made this statement about Jesus: "That's the crux of it. He was too good for them." Our English word *crux*—meaning the decisive point of a problem—comes from the same Latin root that gives us *cross* and *crucify.* The crux of Mary Magdalene's faith in the first century revolved around two places of utter despair: a torturous, wooden cross and a cold, stone grave. Mary M. was *there,* girlfriend. She saw every minute of that fateful Friday unfold.

1a. According to the following verses, what did the people of Galilee and Judea think of Jesus the Nazarene?

Luke 7:16-17

John 6:14

b. Jesus made it very clear to his disciples that his death—and resurrection— were a foregone conclusion. Read **Matthew 17:22-23.** Why do you think his disciples didn't pay attention to the good news at the end of the Lord's prophecy—that he would be raised to life—and instead focused on his impending death?

c. Later in his ministry Christ shared more details of the punishment he would undergo, described in **Luke 18:31-34.** Note the reaction of the disciples in verse 34. What does that suggest to you?

d. Now look at an earlier occasion when Jesus foretold his death, recorded in **Mark 8:31-33.** What does "rebuke" mean, and why do you think Peter responded in this manner?

e. Do you think the disciples might have begun to doubt that Jesus was the true Messiah, or did they simply love him too much to let him go? What motives and emotions do you see at work in this pivotal scene?

f. Now read the parallel account of Jesus' prophecy and Peter's response in **Matthew 16:21-23.** Jot down the specific words Peter used for his rebuke.

g. Let's consider a similar scenario on a personal level: If a loved one were to tell you he or she was facing certain death, what would your reaction be? Would you respond like Peter—"Never!"—or be willing to accept the sad news? What would you say to them?

h. Verses like **Romans 8:11** and **1 Corinthians 6:14** point to the hope of resurrection for those who are members of the body of Christ. How would knowing where loved ones will spend eternity help us accept their impending death…or our own?

These sisters would have gladly carried his cross if anyone had let them.

Liz Curtis Higgs in *Mad Mary,* page 200

2a. After describing the cross that awaited him, Jesus told his followers to be ready to make a sacrifice of their own. Read **Mark 8:34-35.** What did Jesus mean when he said a follower should "take up his cross and follow me"?

b. The Scriptures tell us that one aspect of walking with Christ is to share in his suffering. What do you learn from the following verses about suffering?

Philippians 1:29

2 Thessalonians 1:5

c. How does **1 Peter 4:16** indicate we are to react to such suffering? How far should we be willing to go for our faith? Practically speaking, how might you "take up your cross" as part of your everyday life?

d. Jesus assures us that following in his footsteps will not crush us. Read **Matthew 11:29-30.** Describe a current situation where you resolve to trust in this promise.

e. Read **Mark 15:21.** Since someone else—Simon from Cyrene—physically carried the cross for Jesus on the road to Golgotha, does that alter the meaning or significance of his command to "take up our cross"? What makes you say that?

f. What do the following passages teach you about the connection between the *cross* of Christ and the *joy* of Christ?

John 16:19-22

Hebrews 12:2

Despite his agony, Jesus missed nothing. His gaze caught every tear.

Liz Curtis Higgs in *Mad Mary,* page 201

3a. Read **Matthew 27:55-56.** What brought the women to Golgotha that day? Think through all their possible motivations—practical, spiritual, emotional —adding a bit of explanation for each one listed below.

Mary Magdalene and the other women were there...
to support Jesus because _____

_____

to satisfy their own needs because _____

_____

to encourage one another because _____

_____

to serve as witnesses because _____

_____

to _____ because _____

to _____ because _____

b. The women understood clearly what it meant to *follow* Jesus. Read
Philippians 2:5-8. According to verse 5, we are to pattern ourselves after the
Christ. Verse by verse, then, what did Jesus do and how can you follow his
example in your own life?

	WHAT JESUS DID...	WHAT YOU CAN DO...
Verse 6		
Verse 7		
Verse 8		

c. Of the three steps of obedience you've just listed for yourself, which is the
hardest for you to put into practice? Why?

d. And of those three, which one are you prepared to do right now? Circle that response, then note here one practical step you'll take in that direction this week. (I'll be rooting for you, sis!)

e. In **John 19:25-27** we learn that John, the disciple whom Jesus loved, stood near the cross. None of the other male disciples are mentioned. How would you explain that?

f. Yet **Mark 15:40-41** assures us the women *were* at the cross. Why do you think the gospel writers made very sure that Mary Magdalene's presence was included in their accounts?

Even facing his own demise, he thought of these women, these daughters of Jerusalem, and the misery that awaited them.

Liz Curtis Higgs in *Mad Mary*, page 201

4a. As recorded in **Luke 23:28-30,** on his way to Golgotha, Jesus pointed to the destruction of Jerusalem to come in A.D. 70, some forty years hence. Why did he mention such a thing? Of the following possible explanations, check the one(s) that seems the most likely to you...or add one of your own.

Jesus pointed to the destruction of Jerusalem...

___ to direct their mourning away from him and toward themselves.

___ to encourage them to prepare accordingly.

___ to affirm his prophetic anointing.

___ to _____.

b. Why did you choose the explanation(s) above?

c. Earlier in his ministry, Christ himself wept over Jerusalem. Read **Matthew 23:37-38** and **Luke 19:41-44.** Do you think the women misconstrued the meaning of this prophecy about the destruction of Jerusalem, just as the disciples misunderstood his promises of a coming resurrection? Why or why not?

d. When the early church began to spread the gospel, guess where they started?! Read **Acts 1:8; 5:28;** and **6:7.** Why do you think Christ's followers focused their initial efforts in that particular city? Think through some practical possibilities, then look up **Luke 24:46-48** for the definitive answer.

e. When the city fell years later, how do you think Jesus' final words about Jerusalem impacted the faith of those who had heard his words or heard about his prophecy?

But you did not come down, Jesus. You stayed there. For us.

Liz Curtis Higgs in *Mad Mary*, page 204

5a. The sufferings of Jesus were foreshadowed in great detail centuries before in the Old Testament. Read **Isaiah 53:2-10,** then, verse by verse, make a note of the words and phrases you find in Isaiah's ancient description of the suffering servant that mirror the New Testament accounts of Jesus' life and death.

Verse 2

Verse 3

Verse 4

Verse 5

Verse 6

Verse 7

Verse 8

Verse 9

Verse 10

b. Jesus' excruciating death on the cross must have been the longest six hours in Mary Magdalene's life. Imagine for a moment how Mary M. spent those hours. What did she do? What did she pray? What did she feel? What did she say?

c. How might Jeremiah's words in **Lamentations 5:15-16** express Mary's deepest remorse?

d. Now see yourself at the foot of the cross, as Mary was. Read **James 4:8-10.** What would you do, standing there before the crucified Christ? What would you pray? What would you feel? What would you say?

e. Although we were not on hand for the Lord's death on the cross, we're called to do our best to understand it. How do the truths about Christ's death, as outlined in the following verses, affect the way you live today?

Romans 6:3-5

2 Corinthians 4:10-11

Philippians 3:10-12

f. Reread pages 203-204 in *Mad Mary* where I describe being at my mother's bedside near the end of her days. Have you had a similar experience or watched someone draw his or her last breath? If so, what emotions surfaced? And what regrets came to mind, if any?

g. How might **2 Corinthians 1:3-5** serve as a good means of preparation for such a time of ministry?

h. Was there anything you said that seemed to make things easier for the dying person? What passage of Scripture might you offer as a word of comfort?

i. Did the dying person say anything that made the situation easier for *you?* What does **Matthew 5:4** promise us?

j. How was Mary Magdalene ideally suited for the role of one who stands by the dying?

This darkness was what insurance attorneys call "an act of God."

Liz Curtis Higgs in *Mad Mary,* page 205

6a. We learn in **Isaiah 45:7** that God alone is in charge of darkness. "Darkness" is often used as a metaphor in God's Word. What might darkness represent in the following verses?

Proverbs 4:19

Isaiah 60:2

Matthew 6:22-23

John 12:35-36

b. Now read **Luke 23:44-45.** We know that the darkness at the time of Christ's crucifixion was real, not mere metaphor; an act of God, not a fluke of nature. Do you think the darkness was for God's benefit, his Son's benefit, or the crowd's benefit? Are some things too holy to be seen by man?

c. Read **Mark 15:34** in which Jesus quotes David's words as recorded in **Psalm 22:1.** Could the darkness have signified the total—though temporary—separation of God from his Son? The following verses may help you answer that question. What does each of them tell us about God the Father's involvement in his Son's ministry?

Luke 23:46

John 8:29

2 Corinthians 5:21

d. Consider what happened when the light returned after three long hours of darkness: Relief and a sense of awe must have swept the people. **Psalm 34:4-5** describes how David felt when he turned to God in a frightening moment. Write down all those possible emotions we have when darkness and fear turn to light and hope.

e. Are there murky corners in your own life, beloved, that cry out for the light of Christ to banish their darkness? Take a moment to pray and ask Jesus to show you those dark spots.

f. Now write out **Psalm 18:28** and be assured, my sister, that your Light has come.

For the next three days, his body simply needed a waiting room.

Liz Curtis Higgs in *Mad Mary*, page 209

7a. All four gospel accounts record the burial of Jesus by Joseph of Arimathea. Three of them specifically mention that the women were there. Note all the particular details you find in the following parallel passages.

Matthew 27:59-61

Mark 15:46-47

Luke 23:53-55

John 19:40-42

b. Two of the four passages above mention Mary Magdalene by name; two do not. Should we question the truth of her presence there? Why or why not?

c. At last, we can leave death behind…Easter is upon us! Once again, read the parallel passages for what happened *first* that sacred morning. What important facts do these verses tell us?

Matthew 28:1

Mark 16:1-2

Luke 24:1

John 20:1

d. What motivations—love? curiosity? hope? duty?—do you think brought the women to the tomb on that Sunday morning?

e. Why do you suppose they came at such an *early* hour?

f. What promises do these verses hold for those who seek after God as these women did?

Deuteronomy 4:29

Psalm 14:2

g. What made this anointing of Jesus' body so important to the women? Might their ointment jars simply have been props, a way to gain entrance and see him one more time? Or was this final anointing something significant, and if so, in what way?

h. Read **Mark 16:2-4.** Their concerns about moving the stone were unnecessary. Why? And what does that tell you about God's ability to anticipate our needs?

i. On page 216 of *Mad Mary*, you'll find the statement "No stone is too big for God." What stone does God need to move in your own life in order for you to be set free?

Devotion propelled her toward the tomb, pushing aside her fear.

Liz Curtis Higgs in *Mad Mary,* page 215

8a. Read again chapter 7 in the fictional half of *Mad Mary,* with the following questions in mind. At the start of the chapter, why is Mary Margaret Delaney dragging her feet about going to see her dying pastor at Grant Hospital?

b. If you wondered why Jake's last name was "Stauros," you'll find the answer on page 201 of *Mad Mary.* Throughout chapter 7, what details about Jake's physical body—his appearance, his wounds, his suffering—mirror those of the Christ on Calvary?

c. Jake's dying words are few, but they are meant to parallel two important statements that Jesus made—one to the women, one to his heavenly Father. See if you can find them in the fictional account *and* in the gospel account.

JAKE'S WORDS...	JESUS' WORDS...
Page 112	**Luke 23**
Page 116	**Mark 15**

d. How did vicariously experiencing Mary Delaney's grief help you understand Mary Magdalene's very real suffering so long ago?

e. My intent with "The Story" was not to create a scene identical to the crucifixion, since that was a sacred, once-in-history event. What are some major differences between Mary Delaney's bedside grieving for Jake and Mary Magdalene's vigil at the cross?

Mary's Vigil at the Hospital	Mary M.'s Vigil at the Cross

f. For both women, hope was surely at its lowest ebb. Sometimes our own hopes are crushed when a much-prayed-for dream dies or when God doesn't move in our lives in the way we expected. How do *you* keep hope alive when all seems lost?

FIVE

THE TRYSTED HOUR

Her Discovery

The scenes found in this chapter were the most challenging ones to adapt for "The Story"—how *does* one handle a supernatural resurrection?!—and the most glorious scenes to research and write about for the "The Study." The sheer emotional impact of Mary M.'s reunion with her beloved Teacher—"Rabboni!"—filled my writer's heart to overflowing. Grab your tissues and prepare to meet the risen Savior face to face, just as our sister Mary did long ago.

1a. **Matthew 28:8** tells us Mary Magdalene and the other women "hurried away" to tell the men back in Jerusalem what they'd discovered. On pages 225-226 of *Mad Mary,* I describe them breathlessly tripping over their tunics in their rush to share their exciting news. What do you think empowered these women to speak so boldly?

b. Read **Luke 24:9-11.** How do you think the women felt when the disciples didn't believe them?

c. And why *didn't* the men believe what Mary M. and company had seen? List some possible explanations for their claim that the women were making it all up.

d. What about you, dear one: Are *you* as eager as Mary M. was to tell friends and family about the risen Jesus? What, if anything, is holding you back?

e. Write out **Acts 2:32,** Peter's simple declaration of the truth preached at Pentecost.

f. Although you and I weren't there in person, how are we also "witnesses of the fact"?

g. Would it be easier to proclaim your faith in Christ to a nonbeliever with a group of like-minded sisters accompanying you, or would you rather take that risk alone? What makes you say that?

h. Read Paul's prayer request in **Ephesians 6:19-20,** then fashion his entreaty into your own prayer, in your own words.

i. Worrying about what people will think, say, or do often keeps us from sharing our faith. What truths can you draw from the following passages to bolster your courage to tell others about Christ?

1 Corinthians 2:12-13

2 Corinthians 3:4-6

2 Corinthians 3:12

2 Corinthians 5:18-20

j. If you knew that everyone you shared the Good News with would eagerly receive it, what would you say and do?

[The women] were not running *away* from the tomb so much as they were running *toward* Jerusalem.   Liz Curtis Higgs in *Mad Mary*, page 225

2a. Let's look at two accounts of the many events of Easter morning. Read **Luke 24:1-11** and **John 20:1-11.** How is the scene John describes similar to Luke's version, and how is it dramatically different? Compare the two passages and see if you agree that they are two separate visits to the tomb.

	LUKE 24:1-11	JOHN 20:1-11
Time of day		
Women mentioned		
Location(s) involved		
Discoveries made there		
Men mentioned		
Outcome(s)		

b. It's clear that Mary Magdalene successfully persuaded John and Peter to come see the empty tomb for themselves. What do you think she hoped to accomplish?

c. If the men were skeptical of the women's proclamation, why do you suppose John and Peter did as she asked?

d. What does that tell us about Mary—and about Peter and John?

e. With all we've learned about Mary Magdalene, why do you think she was the one to return to the tomb rather than Joanna or Mary the mother of James or Salome or one of the other women?

You gotta love Mary Magdalene's let's-not-waste-time method of handling things.   Liz Curtis Higgs in *Mad Mary*, page 228

3a. In **John 20:2,** when Mary said, "They have taken the Lord," what "they" was she talking about, do you think? Who were the most likely suspects?

b. Why might they have taken his body in the first place—and where?

c. Perhaps the Pharisees came to mind as possible graverobbers. Read **Matthew 27:62-66** for a brief but telling scene that took place the day after the crucifixion. Whom did the chief priests and the Pharisees suspect might steal the body and to what end?

d. What did these men do to guard against Jesus' body being stolen?

e. When the body was reported missing on Easter morning, the chief priests took action again, even as Mary and the girls headed back to Jerusalem. Read **Matthew 28:11-14.** Whom did the chief priests bribe to lie about the disappearing corpse? And who were those men supposed to blame for it?

f. Clearly the chief priests realized that news of a possible resurrection would build the faith of these disciples. Yet when Mary found a still-empty tomb, her faith in Christ's resurrection seemed to falter. How might you explain that?

g. Sometimes when our hearts are breaking, it's hard to believe that which we can't see. Describe an experience when your own faith was sorely tested.

h. Did you cry out for help, as Mary did? If so, what answers did you receive?

i. How do the following verses strengthen your faith to stand firm and not to falter, even under the most difficult circumstances?

Romans 8:25-28

2 Corinthians 4:7-9

Hearing the truth is one thing. *Knowing* the truth is something else again.

Liz Curtis Higgs in *Mad Mary,* page 228

4a. Read **John 20:10-12.** Life would have been much easier for Mary Magdalene if the angels had stepped forward to confirm things while the men were still there. Why do you think the Men in White waited to reveal themselves until after Peter and John left?

b. It's only fitting that angels would appear at the resurrection, since they also were an integral part of Christ's birth. What role does an angel play in the lives of Christ's family and followers in these familiar passages?

Luke 1:26-30

Matthew 1:19-21

Luke 2:8-11

c. Reread Mary M.'s first recorded encounter with an angel in **Matthew 28:1-5.** Note all the clues that indicate an unsettling experience.

d. Now read **John 20:13.** How do Mary's actions suggest she was neither frightened nor awed by the angels this time? And why might that have been the case?

e. Since the two angels did not bring Mary news but simply asked one ques-
    tion—a question Jesus repeated moments later—why do you think the
    angels were there? Might **Hebrews 1:14** help explain their role in this scene?

Mary Magdalene's heart surely felt as vacant and gaping as the empty tomb
before her.   Liz Curtis Higgs in *Mad Mary*, page 233

5a. Reread **John 20:10-15.** Mary Magdalene certainly did lots of weeping!
    What were those tears all about, do you think? Had she lost more than her
    Lord? Had she lost her faith in his resurrection? her hope for the future? her
    trust in his heavenly Father? Which of those possibilities seems most likely
    and what other losses might she have mourned at this point?

b. In the translation you are using, do the angels in **John 20:13** and the Lord
    in **John 20:15** ask the same question, word for word? What is that question
    and why might they both have asked that?

c. Dozens of scenes in Scripture describe people weeping. Read the following verses, then note *who* was crying and *why.* Were these tears of joy? anguish? sorrow? shame? repentance? supplication? Let the brief details in each verse and your own intuition guide you.

	WHO WAS CRYING	...AND WHY
1 Samuel 1:10-11		
2 Samuel 18:33		
Esther 8:3		
Matthew 26:75		

d. What does crying do for *you,* emotionally speaking?

e. The Lord welcomes our tears, especially if they express heartfelt repentance. Read **Joel 2:12-13.** What are some of the uniquely *spiritual* benefits of weeping?

f. What do the following verses from Psalms tell us about our tears?

Psalm 56:8

Psalm 116:7-9

Psalm 126:5

g. In **John 20:13,** what explanation does Mary Magdalene give for her weeping?

h. Do Mary M.'s countless tears make you think *more* favorably of her, seeing her as empathetic and compassionate, or *less* favorably, seeing her as overly emotional and weak or—heaven forbid!—clueless?

Jesus wants us to grow in faith, and we grow only when we come to the end of ourselves.   Liz Curtis Higgs in *Mad Mary,* page 235

6a. "Clueless" might be the very word that pops into mind when you read **John 20:14!** On pages 237-238 of *Mad Mary,* I offer six possible explanations for Mary's not realizing that the man standing behind her was Jesus. Which of the six sounds the most likely to you, and why? Or does another possibility come to mind?

b. On page 238 of *Mad Mary*, I conclude that Jesus intentionally withheld his identity from Mary. Is that how *you* see it? Why or why not?

c. Skim through the story in **Luke 24:13-31.** The two disciples on the road to Emmaus that day had the very same experience as Mary—confusion (verse 16), then discovery (verse 31). What significance do you see in this hidden, then revealed identity of the risen Christ?

d. That wasn't the first time the disciples were kept from seeing clearly. Read **Luke 9:44-45.** Why do you think the meaning of such an important prophecy was hidden from them? And why were they afraid to ask Jesus about it?

e. **John 1:10** makes a telling statement about "recognizing" Jesus. Write out that verse in your own words here.

f. When did *you* recognize Jesus as Creator and Lord, and why were *you* able to "see" him when not all people do? How might **Matthew 11:25** help answer that question?

g. Mary's experience at the garden tomb that morning suggests that "recognizing" Jesus requires more than opening our eyes. Read **1 Corinthians 2:6-12.** Who or what enables us to clearly see and comprehend all that God has for us?

> The first spoken word of the risen Christ was directed to one of us: "Woman."
>
> Liz Curtis Higgs in *Mad Mary*, page 238

7a. Read **John 20:15.** As we've already noted, Jesus asked Mary exactly the same question the angels had posed moments earlier, but he added a second, more important query. What was that second question and why do you think he asked it?

b. Mary's request this time differed as well. Compare the two verses below. What significant variations do you see?

JOHN 20:13	JOHN 20:15

To whom was she speaking?

JOHN 20:13   JOHN 20:15

What did she say?

Question or statement?

What was her emotional state?

What outcome did she want?

c. Look at the story of Saul (soon to become the apostle Paul) in **Acts 22:6-10.** This passage describes Saul's very personal encounter with Jesus. What do these verses suggest about the Lord's ability to communicate with mankind?

d. Now we come to the high point of Mary's story: **John 20:16.** Jesus says the one word that must have been music to her ears: "Mary." Have you ever had a sense of the Lord's speaking your name? If so, when, where, and why?

e. **John 10:27** assures us we will know the voice of Jesus. Does the thought of hearing Jesus speaking to your heart delight you…or does it trivialize your relationship with a great and mighty God?

f. Mary Magdalene also speaks one word: "Rabboni." She might have cried out "Jesus!" or "Lord!" or "Master!" Why did she use that particular word, do you suppose?

g. What is your favorite title for Jesus? Counselor? King of kings? Savior? Choose one of the many found in Scripture and describe what it means to you in your daily life.

h. Many details throughout the Easter story closely parallel an earlier resurrection, one that involved a different Mary—Mary of Bethany—and her brother, Lazarus. Take a moment to read through the story in **John 11:1-46,** then study the following verses in particular. In each instance, what similarities do you see between these two resurrection stories?

	LAZARUS'S RESURRECTION	JESUS' RESURRECTION
John 11:4		
John 11:11-14		
John 11:17		
John 11:22-23		
John 11:25-26		
John 11:33		

LAZARUS'S RESURRECTION   JESUS' RESURRECTION

John 11:38

John 11:40

John 11:43-44

John 11:45

John 11:46

i. What lessons do you think Jesus was trying to teach his disciples in order to prepare them for his death and resurrection?

The work of a Savior is not to belittle, shame, and ridicule. He comes and finds us where we are and calls us unto himself.

Liz Curtis Higgs in *Mad Mary*, page 240

8a. Read pages 124 through 131 in chapter 8 of *Mad Mary*, keeping these questions in mind. On each page of the text, find just one example of how Mary Delaney's fictional story parallels Mary Magdalene's real-life Easter morning—the time of day, the setting, the individuals present, the words spoken, the actions taken, etc.—then find the verse in the Scripture passages noted that corresponds with the story detail.

AN EASTER MORNING PARALLEL

IN *MAD MARY*	IN LUKE 24:1-11
Page 124	
Page 125	
Page 126	
Page 127	
Page 128	

IN *MAD MARY*	IN JOHN 20:1-16
Page 129	
Page 130	
Page 131	

b. The major missing elements in the modern fictional story are the supernatural ones—heavenly angels, a huge stone being rolled away, and a newly resurrected Christ. Be honest, sis: Were you expecting Jake to suddenly make an appearance in that funeral home?! What if, in some medically feasible manner, Jake had come back to life? How would that have changed things that morning for Mary Margaret Delaney…and for you, dear reader?

c. At any point during your initial reading of *Mad Mary* were you moved, perhaps even to the point of tears? If so, what in Mary's story touched you? What insight do those emotions give you concerning the biblical story?

d. Though Jake died, the words about Jesus that he planted in Mary's heart remained very much alive. Read pages 132 and 133 of *Mad Mary.* What important lesson(s) has she learned?

e. Now think of some difficulty or decision you are currently facing. How might Mary's joyous closing line from a familiar hymn—also found in **Job 19:25**—improve your perspective on your own situation?

SIX

LETTER TO THE WORLD

Her Declaration

Of all the people to whom Jesus might have revealed himself, he chose a woman. *A woman!* If that boggles our twenty-first-century minds, think how those eleven guys must have felt when Mary Magdalene came running back to town with her world-shaking news. Do you hear her sandaled feet pounding the hardened dirt streets of Jerusalem? Sense her breath coming in gasps as she rounds the last corner, her eyes bright with tears of joy? Our hearts swell with anticipation: *Tell us, Mary! What have you seen?*

1a. Mary M. saw Jesus. She heard Jesus. And she touched Jesus…but not for long. Read **John 20:17,** then write out Jesus' first sentence here so we can study it carefully.

 b. Now read his words aloud. What *tone* do you hear in Jesus' voice? What *expression* do you see on his face? What might he have been doing as he said these words—resting a hand on her shoulder or gently pushing her away? Describe the scene as *you* see it.

c. Jesus asks Mary to "stop touching" him, to let go of him. What are some of the things Mary had to let go of that morning in the garden?

d. One of the ways this phrase is translated is "Stop clinging to Me" (NASB). Are those things that you and I often cling to for support—close relationships, the support of friends, a loving spouse—enough to sustain us? What happens when those means of support suddenly disappear?

e. Sometimes we hang on to things we truly need to release. Read the following verses and note what they say to you about hanging on and letting go of specific people, things, and circumstances in your own life.

Jonah 2:8

Mark 7:8

Romans 12:9

f. Throughout biblical history, the Lord asked people to let go of their settled ways and to embrace new lives in new places. Look up the following Old Testament characters. What were they asked to leave behind? And where were they to go?

	What Was He Asked to Leave?	Where Was He Going?

Abram
Genesis 12:1

Lot
Genesis 19:15-17

Moses
Exodus 3:6-10

g. What if God asked you to let go of everything and everyone and trust him completely? Could you do it? If not, what might stop you?

h. What courage can you draw from the following verses to let go and trust the Lord, as Mary did?

Psalm 9:10

Psalm 56:3-4

Proverbs 4:11-13

Having lost him to death, then welcomed him to life, she was *not* about to let go.   Liz Curtis Higgs in *Mad Mary,* page 251

2a. As we've seen, sometimes the Lord asks us to let go of good things in favor of something better. On page 251 of *Mad Mary,* I share a brief example of having to let go of my first spiritual mentors. Has someone filled that role in your life, teaching you, one-on-one, to be a disciple? If so, how did he or she help you grow? If not, in what ways could your walk with Christ be deepened through the help of a personal spiritual coach?

b. Summarize in a word or two the benefits of mentoring—in essence, instruction and encouragement—based on the following verses.

Luke 6:40

John 13:12-17

Ephesians 4:11-13

Hebrews 10:25

c. If you've had a mentor, did a time come when you had to strike out on your own? Why is that a natural part of the mentoring process, and what did you learn from it?

d. Have you learned more in your spiritual life from men or from women? How did their styles of teaching, mentoring, or encouraging differ and how were they the same?

e. The following passages make it clear where the wisdom of a good mentor originates. What do these verses reveal on that subject?

Proverbs 2:6

John 14:23-26

f. In the sentence you copied for question 1a, Jesus explains that he must return to his heavenly Father. What do the following verses indicate about the reasons for his leaving?

John 14:28-31

John 16:7

g. What do the following verses tell us about our mentor—the Counselor, the Comforter, the Holy Spirit—who serves as our personal "spiritual director," and how do these words comfort you?

John 14:16-17

Acts 2:38-39

Mary Magdalene was the first to see him in this sacred transitional state.

Liz Curtis Higgs in *Mad Mary*, page 252

3a. Read **Mark 16:9.** Jesus could have chosen to reveal himself to anyone that sacred morning, but he chose Mary Magdalene. Think of some practical reasons why she was the worst choice, and then explain why she was the best choice.

WORST CHOICE   BEST CHOICE

b. Now let's look at the second half of **John 20:17.** Two short commands
appear in this sentence: *go* and *tell.* This is a familiar idiom from Old
Testament times, as you'll see in **2 Samuel 7:5; Isaiah 38:5;** and **Jeremiah
35:13.** In all these cases, was either *going* or *telling* presented as optional?
What prompts you to draw that conclusion?

c. Did Mary Magdalene *go* and *tell,* as Jesus commanded? What do the following verses reveal about Mary Magdalene's response to her assignment?

Mark 16:10

John 20:18

d. **Mark 16:11** explains clearly what Mary told the disciples…and how they
responded.

Mary told them _____ and _____.

But the disciples _____.

e. Why was that the case? Was she not trustworthy, honest, or faithful? Surely
Proverbs 31:26 aptly describes our honorable Mary M.! How would you
explain their negative response that morning?

f. At various times God calls us to speak truth that may make our listeners—
and us—uncomfortable. Or we may feel we're a "poor choice" for sharing
the message God has given us. Note below what guidance you find for such
situations in the following verses.

Romans 8:33

1 Corinthians 4:2

James 2:5

g. In the middle of page 256 of *Mad Mary*, I point out the key to Mary
Magdalene's story. What is that key? And how does it unlock some important truth for you, sis, and compel you to live out your faith?

h. The following verses teach us about focusing on our mission to share the
gospel rather than getting distracted by how others respond—or don't
respond—to what we tell them. Rewrite each verse as your personal mission
statement, beginning with "I will..."

Romans 1:16

1 Thessalonians 2:3-4

Christ's appearing first to Mary Magdalene was without question his finest assurance to women throughout the ages that he values us.

Liz Curtis Higgs in *Mad Mary*, page 261

4a. How might Christ's ministry and message have changed if Mary of Magdala had been Marcus of Magdala instead? Does the fact that she's a woman enhance the gospel story, detract from it, or not matter at all? What does **Matthew 12:50** suggest?

b. Read **John 4:25-29,** the turning point in the story of the Samaritan woman at the well. Note below the disciples' reaction to her and the woman's response to Jesus' words.

What did the disciples *think?*

And what did they do…or *not* do?

What did the woman do first?

Then where did she go?

To whom did she speak?

And what did she say?

c. How does the previous story relate to Mary Magdalene's go-and-tell experience?

d. In the spirit of balanced teaching, you'll find a wonderful example of a man sharing the gospel with a community and a woman responding to his words in **Acts 16:14-15.** Make a note of all the things that Lydia did after the Lord "opened her heart."

e. A man might just as easily have been there at the tomb that morning, if Jesus had ordained it. At what points in Mary's story does the fact that she's a "she" make a significant difference, do you think?

f. Does it matter to *you* that Mary was a Mary and not a Marcus? Why or
   why not?

The disciples may not have trusted Mary Magdalene as a witness, but
Jesus did.   Liz Curtis Higgs in *Mad Mary*, page 253

5a. A disciple named John wrote **1 John 1:1,** yet the words also fit our Mary
   Magdalene to a T. List all the elements in this verse that mirror Mary's
   experience.

b. Read **John 20:18** again, letting the importance of her news sink into your
   spirit. Have you ever made a Mary kind of declaration to a group of people
   —"I have seen the Lord!"—or something similar? Describe who, where,
   when, and what you said to them.

c. According to **John 4:39,** the Samaritan woman at the well received a positive response to her proclamation. How were *you* received? And how was your *message* received?

d. Maybe you can identify with the words of the apostle John in **John 3:11.** Did your experience make you want to be bolder on another occasion, or do you cringe at the thought of ever again making a fool of yourself like that?

e. How does society look at people who proclaim their faith visibly, noisily, publicly? And how do *you* look at such people?

f. According to **2 Timothy 1:7-8,** how does God ask us to communicate our faith?

g. In addition to proclaiming, "He is risen!" how else can we give witness to our trust in the resurrection? Read **Acts 20:24; Galatians 1:10-12;** and **1 Thessalonians 2:8,** then write out a prayer of commitment to Christ to share the gospel, wherever and whenever.

He wouldn't be returning to that old tomb. Jesus was heaven bound.

Liz Curtis Higgs in *Mad Mary,* page 253

6a. Read **Matthew 28:1-10.** Note the major distinction in verses 9-10—not only did Mary see the risen Christ, but so did the women with her. Do seemingly different versions challenge your faith at all? If so, what does **James 1:5-6** encourage us to do?

b. Reread my own explanation of the differing accounts in the middle of page 260 in *Mad Mary.* How might *you* reconcile those apparent story variations in your own mind?

c. Could you explain these apparent discrepancies to others, if the subject came up? (However tempting, please don't offer them **Hebrews 5:11** as your explanation!) What *would* you say?

d. What do the following verses reveal about the trustworthiness of God's Word?

Psalm 19:8-9

Psalm 119:152

Proverbs 30:5

Mary Magdalene...was the prime minister of information that Easter morning.

Liz Curtis Higgs in *Mad Mary*, page 255

7a. Read **1 Peter 1:8-9.** In what ways does this verse describe how you feel about the risen Christ, even though you have not physically seen him with your own eyes, as Mary Magdalene did?

b. Though she may have been counted among the women mentioned in **Acts 1:14,** Mary M. quietly disappears from Scripture after her big morning at the garden tomb. In what ways might she have continued to exert a positive influence on the early church…and on the church today?

c. Read page 263 in *Mad Mary.* How does the listing of women from **Romans 16** encourage you?

d. Can you imagine your own name alongside Phoebe's and Priscilla's? Why or why not?

e. Read the following verses, then record below how you intend to answer their challenge by ministering to others.

Colossians 1:10-12

Colossians 3:23-24

Hebrews 6:10-12

f. Read **Psalm 112:1-6.** How will you be remembered among your sisters in Christ when you are gone?

g. And what legacy of faith will you leave behind for your loved ones? How can you adapt the instructions in **Deuteronomy 11:18-21** for your twenty-first-century household?

When you are sold out to God, you cannot *not* go and tell.

Liz Curtis Higgs in *Mad Mary*, page 256

8a. Read pages 270-271 of *Mad Mary*, an encore appearance by Mary Margaret Delaney. Based on this brief scene, what are some of the many lessons our contemporary Mary clearly learned on her journey?

b. Now that we've studied both Marys—ancient and modern, real and fictional—from every angle, what lesson has Mary Magdalene taught you above all others?

c. Can you say with Mary Delaney—right now, out loud—"I see the Christ alive in me"? Put down this workbook and do it! How did that announcement make you feel?

d. If you were to begin each day with that wondrous declaration, how would it affect…

your interactions with others?

your response to life's challenges?

your view of yourself and your role in God's kingdom?

e. Are you prepared to *go* and *tell,* as both Marys did? Is anything stopping you?

f. If you *are* ready, who will be the next person to hear the Good News from your lips?

ONE MORE THING

Oh, that Mary M. Isn't she something?

What an honor it has been to introduce you to my favorite woman—Bad Girl *or* Good!—from the pages of Scripture. My prayer, throughout the long process of researching and writing *Mad Mary*, was that my reader—yes, *you*, sis—might come to know not only Mary Magdalene, but also the Lord whom Mary loved and served with her whole heart. You'd be hard-pressed to find a better role model anywhere.

I hope this workbook in particular allowed you to fully grasp the timeless truths found in Mary's story and to linger in God's Word so that he might teach you, through the power of his Holy Spirit, what it means to be a disciple of the risen Christ.

Easter will never be the same for me after studying Mary's life of dedication, then despair, then discovery, then declaration. How thrilling to say without hesitation, "I have seen the Lord!" Have *you* seen him, beloved? Then it's time to "go and tell" the world as Mary M. did and watch him transform lives before your very eyes.

As with all my Bad Girls projects, Rebecca Price, Laura Barker, Carol Bartley, and Stephanie Terry kindly read the manuscript for this workbook and offered exceptional feedback. And where would I be without my husband, Bill? He not only sifted through every reference and every question before giving them his scholarly stamp of approval, he also made sure my cupboard was stocked with plenty of Scottish shortbread and Earl Gray tea. A gem of a man, this.

When you're ready for another Lizzie-style Bible study, *Bad Girls of the Bible* and *Really Bad Girls of the Bible* are waiting at a bookstore near you. Those best-selling books, their companion workbooks, and the hourlong VHS videos that go with them might be just the things for your next women's gathering, large or small.

A final confession: Even after sixteen years of speaking and nineteen published books, I have much to learn and far to go in my walk with Jesus. I definitely don't have all the answers—but I'm grateful for One who does. Bless you for being part of my growing process by letting me know, by post or e-mail, what your time with *Mad Mary* has meant to you:

Liz@LizCurtisHiggs.com
Liz Curtis Higgs
P.O. Box 43577
Louisville, KY 40253-0577

I hope we meet across the page again soon. Until then, go and tell the world the Good News, my sister!

To learn more about WaterBrook Press and view
our catalog of products, log on to our Web site:
www.waterbrookpress.com

WATERBROOK
PRESS